is dynamic and uncertain, which does not cre
conditions for stable and sustainable increases in p

* This problem may be exacerbated by co...peution for
Russian oil by third parties, particularly China, India, Japan and
the USA, all of whom have begun to show an active interest in
Russian oil. High competition for finite resources is likely both
to drive up prices and reduce the amount of Russian oil available
to the EU.

Contents

Russian Oil and EU Energy Security

Dr. Andrew Monaghan

Introduction

The security of energy supplies has become a major issue for the EU. Imports account for approximately 50% of the EU's energy consumption, a figure expected to rise to some 70% in 2030, and in the case of oil products to 90%.[1] Finding stable sources to support this increase is a key priority. The proximity of Russia, one of the world's leading producers and suppliers of oil, suggests that it is logical to establish a mutually beneficial energy relationship with it. And indeed, Russia is considered the EU's 'most important supplier of fossil fuels ... being in some ways the most promising ... alternative to the Middle East as energy supplier to Europe'.[2] An EU-Russia energy dialogue has developed since 2000, one officially considered by the EU to have developed into a 'true partnership which today offers wider prospects which go beyond the narrow questions of energy trade, extending to transport-related problems and to the environmental impact of the energy sector'.[3]

However, this (increasing) dependence on energy imports generates a number of problems, since the exhaustion – or even scarcity – of energy supplies would have serious ramifications for industries and societies. Moreover, it is equated with vulnerability and greater power accorded to external suppliers. The EU's Green Paper on energy security noted that 'in the present situation, we are less and less able to overcome our vulnerability ... we suffer from a singular lack of means for negotiation and pressure ... our room for manoeuvre is limited, whether the crisis be acute or long-term'.[4] As such, energy security is considered a 'special concern' in the EU's Security Strategy.[5]

Particular unease has recently been voiced that the EU could find itself increasingly at the mercy of an ever more authoritarian Russia which might use its control over a large share of the EU's energy imports as a diplomatic lever against it. As one high-profile analysis has phrased it, the hallmarks of President Putin's power are the curtailment of liberty and pluralism at home and the 'single-minded pursuit of *realpolitik* by energy blackmail' abroad.[6] Such concerns have gained a stronger foothold in debates perhaps largely because of the difficulties experienced in the Russia-EU relationship in the last two years, the slow and difficult progress in the energy dialogue and as a result of Poland and Germany being affected by energy shortages in 2004 due to Russia cutting off energy exports to Belarus, through which much of the EU's energy is transported.

This has become a real problem in Western European and Russian public discourse and has filtered into political circles. The high-profile nature of such worries was again illustrated following the EU-Russia summit of October 2005, when much attention was focused on EU dependency on Russian energy and how this would undermine the EU's ability to criticise Russia. Whatever reservations they may have about political developments in today's Russia, the Europeans have a 'strong incentive to be tactful' because of the energy dependence, one high-profile newspaper has claimed.[7]

1

Russian Oil and EU Energy Security
Conflict Studies Research Centre
ISBN 1-905058-48-9
November 2005

Dr Andrew Monaghan

And there has been the occasional mention of such a potential from among the Russian elite. Vitaliy Tret'yakov, a Professor in MGIMO and a member of Russia's high-profile Council on Foreign and Defence Policy (SVOP),[8] has seemingly argued that Russia might use its oil exports to ensure that Russia is treated with respect as one of the European powers without being forced to work for such status. Russia should enjoy all the privileges extended to EU members, he argued, otherwise it would not offer the EU any concessions to them where the volumes of and prices for oil are concerned.[9] Others in business circles, such as Vagit Alekperov, the President of LUKOIL, have also hinted that states whose oil sector is largely owned by Russian companies such as Bulgaria would be unlikely to pursue an anti-Russian foreign policy.[10] Finally, politicians such as Grigory Yavlinskiy have on occasion asserted that oil is for Putin what nuclear warheads were to the USSR.[11]

This has led to analysts questioning whether the EU could rely on Russia as an energy supplier.[12] Such concerns seem to have filtered through to the Russian body politic. Speaking in June 2005, Dmitri Rogozin argued that the EU has an "oil phobia" about Russia, a phobia that Russia will use energy as a political weapon against the EU.[13] Others have noted that there is growing frustration with EU member states among Russian official circles about such concerns.[14]

This paper examines the EU's increasing dependence on imported Russian oil, addressing the origins of the "oil phobia". Although the "phobia" of Russia using oil exports as a lever is overplayed, there are problems that the EU needs to consider while planning its energy security. The paper first looks at definitions of energy security, before turning to examine the evidence of Russia using its oil exports as a diplomatic "weapon". Subsequently, the paper assesses the EU-Russia relationship, looking at the interdependent nature of the relationship. Finally, prospective problems are looked at, including the limits of Russian oil production and transport and competition for Russian oil from other states.

Energy Security

Energy security is maintained by strategic planning to ensure diversity of fuel, diversity of supply source, and efficiency and flexibility in the energy sector. Defining threats to energy security, however, is more difficult, since it is a wide-ranging concept covering many aspects, including access to fuel (at acceptable prices), safe transit and processing of the fuel, and protection of the environment and resources.[15] Defining energy security more clearly is also complicated by the variety of views of what is at stake. To some it means protecting against politically induced supply disruptions (i.e. the supplier "turning off the taps") or technically induced supply problems (accident or breakdown), to others it is facing the challenges of terrorism,[16] and to yet others, it means addressing the issue of global warming by changing consumption patterns.[17]

For convenience here, it can be divided into two interlinked dimensions – geological and political. For many, energy security is a long-term practical, geological issue, based on the sustainability of production. There is a debate among big business, geologists and analysts about the future of global reserves. The "peak" camp, consisting mainly of geologists and engineers, argues that there are limits to oil supplies, and questions the sustainability of global production. The camp argues that the world is arriving at peak production which will soon plateau and then decline. It also argues that improvements in technology mean that reservoirs are depleted more quickly – there has been little investment in research and development to facilitate new technological leaps to access more oil.[18]

Others, however, particularly economists, are more optimistic, arguing that the level of oil in the ground, although limited, is not fixed. Improvements in technology mean that more production will be possible. They point to the fact that the ultimate recoverable resource base has grown consistently, despite the fact that world consumption has increased. Many areas of the world remain under-developed and under-explored – there is now, for example, underwater exploration at depths that were unimaginable a decade ago.[19]

The second dimension of energy security is clearly framed by the United Kingdom's energy security strategy. It notes that although 'world reserves are widely assessed to be more than sufficient to meet projected demand for oil ... over the next few decades, provided national and international frameworks allow them to be developed', by 2020 around 50% of total oil demand will be 'met by countries with a significant potential risk of internal instability'.[20] In fact, domestic political stability is a pivotal issue – although there are 130 un-drilled prospects in Iraq (an example cited by optimists underlining the potential for exploration); continuing instability following the Iraq war clearly poses problems for developing them efficiently. Equally, Russia has great potential as an oil supplier – but uncertainty over the foreign investment and political climate in Russia jeopardises the inflow of modern technology to facilitate, let alone maximise, production.[21]

These elements can be drawn together to establish two key tenets originally mentioned for enhancing energy security in the view of consumers – the limitation of vulnerability to disruption given the increasing dependence on imported oil from unstable areas and the provision of adequate supply for increased demand at reasonable prices.[22]

But here one caveat should be noted with regard to the cost of oil and the risk of oil price volatility. Oil is a fungible commodity. This means that oil prices are governed by world market conditions, rather than any given state – Russian oil may rise in cost because of events in Venezuela, for instance, or the USA, irrespective of any political machinations in Moscow. Price volatility poses concern, not least because a major rise in prices affects key industries (and citizens' heating bills). It is a problem since diversification of supplies is helpful but does not guarantee safety – even states which do not import oil have to meet higher prices. Thus governments concerned about their energy security must in the end face the necessity of enhancing domestic efficiency and reducing fossil energy use – of weaning themselves off their oil addiction, as one newspaper has phrased it.[23]

Most definitions of energy security only examine the consumer's side, without examining that of the producer, and how these different understandings may interlink or be compared – but this is a key element of the energy security debate. Many producer concerns appear similar to those of the consumer, of course – pipeline security is a good example. Both sides need secure transit facilities. But there are differences that will influence Russia's position in the world energy market and inevitably the Russia-EU energy relationship. First, there is clearly a different perspective concerning energy prices – an exporter quite evidently seeks higher prices than an importer. A fall in oil prices is beneficial to the consumer's energy security, but threatens that of a producer. This has three particular ramifications for Russia.

First, the Russian economy has been buoyed by high oil prices – a reduction in oil prices would have major knock-on effects on the Russian economy. Second, it would both reduce the income from stable exports such as those to Europe (the

Dr Andrew Monaghan

growth of oil exports was the main source of Russian GDP growth from 2002-4), and also impact on transit, thereby increasing dependence on fewer markets. Just as having fewer sources undermines consumer security, so having fewer markets undermines producer security. Currently, for example, due to the high prices of oil, Russia can transport oil by train to China, despite this being a very expensive mode of transit – adding an extra $5-7 per barrel. Should oil prices fall, however, it will no longer be economically viable even for a China desperate for oil. Russia would not only lose income but a market until pipelines can be completed.[24] But these also are expensive to build, and a reduction in income would undermine the financial case for construction. This is discussed in more depth below.

Second, the producer also needs secure and reliable export facilities. Exporting via foreign states increases the price and is vulnerable to their political perspective, creating a dependence on that state for the export of a central element of the state's economy. If a consumer fears the supplier "turning off the taps", a supplier fears a blockage in the supply system, or being held to ransom by transit states.

Third, one of the key elements of energy security is perception. John Roberts, an energy analyst with Platt's, a global energy information service, notes that fears about energy security are real, although they may not be justified. Other experts concur, arguing that security amounts to a feeling – comfort is the point. Robert Skinner, Director of the Oxford Energy Institute, argues that context is important to this feeling, particularly the state of global markets, state of regional political stability and above all the nature of the relationship at any particular time between the buyer and seller of an energy commodity.[25]

And energy security lends itself very well to a feeling of vulnerability in the west – an immediate shortage of oil would pose major problems for Western economies and serious domestic political questions. An immediate shortage of gas, particularly in cold northern areas, would pose serious problems for heating costs; one of oil for transport costs. Such fears are justifiable in that they require serious planning, but are also vulnerable to hyperbole in the public press and political statements and problems can become unrealistically magnified.

A cause of this is the uncertainty surrounding energy, the lack of hard numbers and evidence and the shifting sands in state-private sector relations in many producing states. As many in the peak and optimist camp note, we simply do not know how much oil is in the ground, nor how much of this uncertain amount is economically viable – there are proved, possible and probable reserves.[26] Numbers are at best informed estimations. Moreover, statistics are variously measured – there are differing systems of quantification.[27] This is compounded by high levels of business and state secrecy surrounding the energy sector. Although publications such as the BP Annual Statistical Review provide good information, it is also true that accurate knowledge is a highly profitable business asset and guarded as such. This is not only the case in business – Moscow recently announced that Russian reserves are a state secret. Much planning and negotiation goes on behind closed doors.[28] Finally, it should be noted that figures are often seriously manipulated or ignored completely in texts highlighting soaring demand and falling production. Manipulation and vague but dramatic scenario portrayal serve only to maximise sensitivity.

This problem is exacerbated by uncertainty about specifically foreign imports and producers. As Skinner has noted, the "us and them" approach to energy security – "them" being the foreign producers – is a recurrent theme in energy security. However, as Skinner asks, is viewing energy security in terms that imply mistrust a helpful starting point? Often these "unreliable foreigners" are not as untrustworthy as they might appear – they need the relationship as much as the consuming states. Viewed globally, the empirical record shows that most oil and gas supply interruptions did not involve foreign producers cutting off other countries' consumers. Skinner points out that far more frequently, consumer countries have reduced supply through sanctions and boycotts against oil producers.[29] Nonetheless, this is a particularly relevant point concerning Russia and the widespread distrust of Russia.

Russian Use of the Energy "Weapon"

Much of the suspicion that Russia would use its energy resources as a negotiation tool by "turning off the taps" draws on evidence from Russia's relationships with former Soviet states. According to a number of analysts, Russia has 'systematically' attempted to use energy means as a lever to limit the autonomy and shape the foreign policies and particularly change the western orientations of Newly Independent States (NIS), or as a means of undermining the new political and economic systems in Eastern and Central Europe'. Russia 'does not hesitate to use its economic power and in the energy field, especially with respect to the new EU members', and directs cut-offs at states, using oil and gas to pressurise the policies of Belarus, Ukraine and Moldova'. The 'cost of the heavy dependence of these states on Russian energy is obvious to policymakers in both states (Belarus and Ukraine) – reduced political autonomy'. Thus according to one analyst, 'current Russian policies pose a threat to the development of transparent democratic governments and free market policies in those countries that depend on Russia for their energy resources … energy is more easily deployable for power projection than nuclear weapons'.[30]

It is important to note that with cut-offs to Belarus or the Ukraine, for what ever reason they are made, there has been a knock-on impact on Polish and German reserves.[31] Therefore, this is an issue which warrants attention at least in this respect. Nonetheless, the EU should make a distinction between a knock-on effect and a desired outcome. Indeed, a number of points should be clarified about Russia's use of the energy "weapon". First, those who assert these attempts argue that they were ineffective. By treating Russia as a security threat, Ukraine did not give in to Russian demands, for instance.[32]

Second, it is too great a leap to make comparisons between the NIS and the EU: the context is wholly different. One of the main problems for NIS is that they are not just dependent on Russian energy, but cheap Russian energy – Ukraine, for example, could not afford alternative supplies.[33] Geographically, also, it is difficult for the NIS to find different suppliers – to varying but significant degrees they are all linked by rail, pipelines and refineries to Russian energy.[34] The EU, however, is a very different actor. It is much wealthier and can diversify its supply more readily: the "dependency" argument is less applicable. Indeed, Russia is already a diversification for the EU.

Finally, the "weapon" argument needs to be checked more rigorously in three ways. Some analysts note that Russia cannot effectively use the energy lever against western former soviet states, since this affects supplies to Western Europe. Moreover, NIS have proven particularly adept at using the fact that Russia depends on them to export its oil and gas against Russia itself. This is not only by charging Russia transit fees:[35] most pipeline cut offs have been made by transit states. Some analysts suggest that the transit states are also good at playing the producer and consumer against each other for their own benefit. The US, for instance, 'found itself at a loss when after two years of financing repayment of Ukraine's energy bills to Russia, new debt appeared to be mounting as rapidly as it had been retired'.[36] Simply put, the EU needs to be more clear about the specifics of claims being made against Russia using energy exports as a "weapon".

Furthermore, Russia's use of energy as a political tool is open to question in two ways. First, a number of analysts have argued that although there are links between some of the major private companies and the state, Russian oil companies have been privatised. Despite the YUKOS affair, most of them remain so. This means that although they should not go beyond certain domestic political limits, the Russian government is not in a position to use them as foreign policy instruments, since they are not under full state control.[37] This point can be debated. Many private Russian firms may well find it convenient to work with the Russian state when it suits them. The point is that, despite the increased efforts by the state to enhance vertical authority, Russia's decision-making processes cannot simply be reduced to state authority – they are complex, dynamic and need much more investigation. As with many other dimensions of Russian foreign and security policy, the link between state desires and the actions of the majority of Russian oil companies is not that direct.[38] The influence of the companies on the state must also be considered in this equation.

Second, a number of energy experts have noted that there have been no clear examples of purely political use of energy cut offs by Russia.[39] Cut offs almost invariably had economic reasons, such as the non-payment of debts, or technical reasons, such as accident.[40] This is certainly an issue that the EU will need to address – but in the appropriate circumstances of economic debt or technical problem rather than a politically motivated attack.

EU-Russia energy dialogue

The EU-Russia energy dialogue was launched in 2000 (in the context of the EU's Green Paper on Energy Security) on the initiative of Presidents Chirac and Putin and the then-Commissioner Prodi, in the recognition that Russia and the EU are natural partners in the energy sector and given their mutual interests in enhancing the overall energy security of the continent. The objective was to provide a forum for the discussion of all questions of common interest in the energy sector and bind Russia and the EU into a closer relationship.

Senior officials on both sides were appointed to oversee the dialogue,[41] and some positive progress has been made in the relationship. Working groups have met regularly;[42] and a Technology Centre was established in November 2002 for the exchange of information and the promotion of new energy technology to support Russia in accelerating the development of the oil and gas sectors. The centre has organised round table discussions on the exploitation of Russian reserves and improvements in Russian oil refining. Lately, the British presidency of the EU during the second half of 2005 has sought to prioritise the energy relationship and add a new dynamism to the dialogue. A Permanent Partnership Council (PPC) meeting was held on 3rd October 2005 at which plans and aims were agreed and a framework for achieving these plans established. This has created more structure to the relationship, with a wider set of interlocutors to create new vested interests. The dialogue is now broader, including business and political authorities from Russia and the EU, represented in four thematic groups focusing on investment, infrastructure, trade and energy efficiency. Each of these groups has met twice since June 2005.[43]

Officially, the dialogue is considered to have had positive results, opening the way to European investment in the Russian energy market and as a forum for tackling difficulties. 'Frank and open discussions have already permitted substantial progress to be made' and the dialogue has developed into a true partnership which today offers wider prospects which go beyond the narrow questions of energy trade.[44] The EU has been at particular pains to point out that there is a strong common interest in the energy sector. Repeatedly, the EU states that Russia has been a reliable supplier, always respecting the dates, amounts and prices agreed even during periods of internal political turbulence or dramatic world developments.[45] Interviews also suggest that Russia has officially sought to be a cooperative partner: there have been no signs from Russian executive officials about Russia using its energy resources as a lever over the EU. Rather the opposite, according to EU officials and experts, who have pointed out that Russia has sought to be a good supplier.[46]

Yet if it is based in the common recognition of the realities of the importance of the relationship, a series of problems and differences underlie the relationship. Positive measures remain marginal, and the dialogue has been held up by differing interpretations and priorities. Russia seeks support to modernise its energy sector and protect itself, while the EU wants reform and the opening of the Russian market through the creation of a positive business climate.[47]

In fact, official accounts and expert analysis suggest that it is Russia which has more concerns about the future of the energy relationship, rather than the EU. This is for a number of reasons, the first of which is that if the development of the EU's internal market is creating opportunities for Russia by building the world's largest and most integrated energy market in its immediate periphery, it also creates concerns. Russian analysts argue that the European Commission will show 'maximum tenacity and assume a hard stance' in its desire to safeguard EU interests. Russia's dialogue with such an entity would only prove successful if the various interests in Russia reach a solid consensus defining exactly what Russia's interests in the energy sector as a whole are. Such real and lasting consensus is likely to be difficult to achieve, and the answers to many questions remain unclear – what is to be the goal of Russia's energy policy in Europe? What are the limitations and risks involved? How can export revenues be best used for Russia's development? The analysts argue that it is still necessary to develop export priorities, routes, projected costs and sources of finance – no detailed elaboration of specific plans exists.[48] Such lack of consensus undermines the Russian negotiating position.[49]

This point is emphasised by those who argue that the objective of the energy relationship is to put pressure on Russia to initiate reform within its energy sector, particularly with regard to domestic prices. The EU, they argue, has sought to pressurise Russia to bring its domestic prices closer to those of the world market. Official statements reflect such concern: President Putin argued in 2003 that 'the EU will not succeed in twisting Russia's arm in its desire to achieve a sharp hike in fuel prices'. Moscow has argued that it will be politically unrealistic to raise prices sharply to poor consumers and second that energy resources are Russia's natural competitive advantage, and that it will be difficult for Russian enterprises should prices be so raised.[50] But the EU and member states should realise that it will be as difficult for Moscow to impose such increasing costs on Russian businesses and population (who are used to negligible energy costs) as it will be for Western governments to impose more efficient and particularly less domestic energy use on their own populations.

There are also signs that Russia is concerned about its access to this integrated market and that the EU has imposed limits on energy imports from Russia. Although the EU has repeatedly denied this, arguing that since the EU seeks help from Russia to diversify its fossil fuel supplies it is inconceivable that the EU should impose quantitive restrictions on its imports,[51] Russian concern continues.

Finally, there are concerns in Russia that the EU's demand will not grow significantly in any case and the market is restricted. Indeed, many note that oil consumption in Europe is not growing substantially. A paper presented by Russian analysts to a discussion group attended by Russia's leading energy specialists, for example, noted that 'during the last 25 years, Europe has rapidly shifted from the consumption of traditional fuels, primarily coal and oil to natural gas and to a lesser degree, nuclear energy'. Thus, between 1973 and 2000, the share of oil in Europe's energy - consumption dropped from 60 to 40%. Another expert noted that oil demand growth in the EU 27 (to include Bulgaria and Romania) in 2015, as compared to 2000 would be minus 12.5%. Thus even the development to the Baltic pipeline system has a limited strategic perspective for Russia, since it is limited purely to this stagnating European market.[52]

Western analysts also note that EU oil demand is flat, because the population is stable, it is more efficient at using oil and is moving away from oil use. Indeed, one author has argued that the EU is leading the world in the shift to renewable sources of energy and is 'far ahead of the USA and Asia in the race to end its dependence on natural resources to make it the first continent of energy independence'.[53] Less exuberant, but providing the foundations for such arguments, BP's Annual Statistical Review suggests that oil consumption in Europe and Eurasia has hardly increased since 1994 – from 19.8 million barrels to 20 million barrels per day (mbpd). Although the new member states' consumption has increased slightly, the share of the main EU states has been stable or decreasing. The EU 25's total consumption has increased just slightly from 13.5 to 14.6mpbd. EU consumption of middle distillates, which forms the majority of consumption, has risen from 5.3 to 6.6, but that of gasolines has dropped from 3.8mpbd in 1994 to 3.5 and fuel oil from 1.95mbpd to 1.65. The overall increase from 2003 to 2004 was just 0.7%. Overall growth is not just slow but fluctuating – slow but steady growth from 1994 to 1998 almost stopped in 1999, before decreasing in 2000. Renewed growth in 2001 was again followed by a decrease in 2002. 2004's consumption was approximately that of 2001.[54] Even if North Sea and other "domestic" EU oil production is falling, thereby increasing the need for imports, anaemic growth in its major consumer market cannot but give cause for concern in a producing state that seeks to export as much as possible.[55]

In fact, if Russia is an important supplier of oil to Europe, it is also a marginal one, and Europe's "dependence" on Russian oil is questionable.[56] Even analysts who argue that the EU is vulnerable to Russian machinations note that in 1999, the EU imported 16% of its oil from Russia, but that this had dropped to circa 15-14%. Europe 'receives the lion's share of Russian oil exports and Russia's importance will only grow further', the authors argue. They then make comparisons with the Cold War period, when NATO states were recommended to have a maximum of 10% dependence on the USSR for certain commodities, a figure which 'serves as an indication of what sometimes is considered to be the level where dependence makes possible usage of energy leverage for political or economic purposes'.[57]

The comparison with the USSR is illuminating both on factual grounds and also by illustrating the atmosphere behind the debate. Yet the confrontation of the Cold War is finished. Russia and the EU have a strategic partnership, however flawed:

the conditions have changed dramatically. Moreover, the same statistics can be read in a different way – if the EU's share of Russian exports has doubled since 1991 ('receiving the lion's share' of Russian oil exports), while Russia's share of the EU's total oil import *decreases*, this suggests that Russia is more dependent on the EU market than the EU on Russian oil.

Revenues from oil exports, particularly to Western Europe as the primary consumer, are simply too important to the Russian economy. Russia is not only currently dependent on its West European market, it is also dependent on Eastern and Central European transit routes. The main pipelines flow west to Europe, and the infrastructure for oil export to the east is still underdeveloped. Russia is currently tied to European consumers, and considers itself vulnerable both to economic and political blackmail since it has to export the majority of its produce through other states.[58] Thus, if the EU is "dependent" on Russian oil (and dependence is a generous term), it is clearly a mutual dependence, one where Russia is currently more dependent on the EU. It is therefore highly unlikely to cut off its oil exports to the EU in an effort to exert diplomatic leverage.[59]

Indeed, from the Russian perspective, it seems that they are vulnerable to energy leverage and the dangers of dependency on the EU. According to one analyst, there are fears that the EU will seek to exert pressure on Moscow and seek other sources before Russia can develop other markets. These fears result in the stoking of fears of retaliation if alternative deals are pursued by the EU.[60] Here lies a potential problem. Until recently, experts noted that the energy relationship had hardly spilled over in ways one might expect into the political dialogue in terms of influencing EU positions.[61] However, if both sides become nervous about their energy security, diversification away from each other is the answer. This creates an "energy security dilemma".[62]

Russian Oil Production: Reserves and Transport Capabilities

Russia is a perfect model of the debate between the "peak" and "optimist" camps. On one hand, Russia superficially has vast reserves, and a great potential for exporting them. But on the other, sceptics argue that Russian oil may not have the 'staying power' hoped for by consumers.[63] This is predominantly for two interconnected reasons – Russian geology and geography on one hand; its effective exploitation on the other.

Russia is the world's second largest oil producer. Russia's discovered and projected oil reserves are among the largest on earth and Western Siberia is the world's richest hydrocarbon province.[64] There are also high expectations of potentially enormous reserves in other regions which have yet to be exploited or even fully explored, such as East Siberia, the Komi Republic, Nenets Autonomous Okrug and the Barents region.[65] Hopes about the future possibilities of Russian reserves have been further driven by a major increase in production and export since the late 1990s.[66] Although production fluctuated during the mid-to-late 1990s,[67] it has increased dramatically since 2000. Production in 2000 was 6.5mbpd; this has risen to 9.3 in 2004. 2004's figure represented growth of 8.9% over that of 2003.[68] Virtually all of this increase was exported.[69] Russian experts and officials are divided about 2005 production, some predicting a further 6-8% increase, others, particularly Transneft the State transport monopoly, expect 4%. A September to September stagnation, caused in large part by a dramatic increase in tax on oil production and exports, however, has been followed by another leap in production to a new post-Soviet high of 9.53mbpd.[70]

A major reason for this acceleration in production has been the exploitation of "old" oil – oil which was explored and easily accessible during the 1980s and 1990s because it was either bypassed by less efficient production techniques or because of the economic disarray of the 1990s. By exploiting these opportunities, Russian producers increased production in a large number of previously neglected post-peak fields.[71] A number of further factors facilitated the exploitation of this old oil since 1999, including the devaluation of the ruble in 1998 (thereby making it more internationally competitive), greater political stability under President Putin, the attitudes of big business, who sought to profit from a favourable situation and high oil prices, which has generated money to invest.[72]

However, according to one expert, if the increase in production since the late 1990s was an 'extraordinary engineering and managerial accomplishment ... much of the gain was ephemeral and not subject to either extension or repetition'.[73] Indeed, conditions in Russia for the development of a stable oil sector with long-term accelerated growth prospects are not propitious, and a number of experts and officials are predicting the quick depletion of Russian oil reserves.[74]

Some Russian official's talk of a sharp downturn in production and the severe deterioration of the oil reserves base – Yuri Trutnev, Minister of Natural Resources, for example, has stated that exploration is urgently needed to prevent a levelling off or even fall in Western Siberian output after 2010.[75] Shmal has also stated that Russia's oil exports are in danger unless a programme of geological exploration of new deposits is introduced. 'Unless the government and public stop thinking about oil and gas as some magic wand that works and works and doesn't ask to eat, soon Russia will lose its export capacities'. The only solution, he argued, is to establish a wide programme of geological exploration and tapping of new deposits.[76]

Western energy experts have pointed to Russia's mounting dependence on a small number of very large fields, which are considered moderately to very mature. Although these may rise again in production, it is unlikely that they would revisit previous peaks. This does not necessarily mean that shortages are immediate. Experts note that reserves have not been fully exploited, with oil remaining in the flanks of fields or at deeper levels than those currently being developed and that levels of production can therefore be maintained for several years based on fields presently operating.[77]

However, it does raise the profile of two problems. First, the dependence on a decreasing number of large fields means that the oil sector is fragile and vulnerable to accident. A field accident which shut down 50% of the production of one large field could have an impact on national production.[78] Second, important sources of growth in the long term are new fields – which are not yet producing and are hundreds of miles from infrastructure. There is continuing uncertainty about when production will begin. Indeed, geographic constraints pose serious problems for the economic exploitation of Russian oil: many of the Russian reservoirs still to be explored and exploited are in very harsh climates and are thousands of miles from the nearest markets. These two factors raise production and transportation capital costs significantly. One estimate suggests that these factors raise the cost of production dramatically compared to other producers: a barrel costs on average $1-1.5 in the Middle East to produce, but $12-14 in Russia. Russia also then has to pay extra to transport the oil to its markets.[79] Thus, some Russian oil will be beyond the reach of technology for the foreseeable future; and more will be viable only in an environment of sustained high oil prices.[80]

There are a number of limits to potential future growth, including the impact of insufficient export capacity, low oil prices, political interference and voluntary restraint.[81] Technical problems with the oil export are evident, particularly regarding capacity. In many areas, particularly those discovered but still to be produced, transport is either insufficient or non-existent.[82] Furthermore, bottlenecks in the port and pipeline system mean that export capacity is incapable of meeting the ambitions of producers.[83] The US Department of Energy estimates that of the 7 mbpd for export, only 4 million are exported by trunk pipeline, the rest is transported by rail and barge. Thus, unless there is significant investment to expand the pipeline infrastructure, only non-pipeline exports will be able to grow in the near future. This poses concerns for Russia, however – as noted above, Russian export is more vulnerable to the vagaries of oil prices. Should they fall (one estimate suggests to below $20/barrel), rail and river transport becomes uneconomic.[84] Yet, as noted above, currently only rail routes supply East Asia.[85]

It should be noted here though, that other authorities disagree about the short-term possibilities – the International Energy Agency (IEA)[86] noted in 2004 that the list of pipeline and export terminal expansions planned until 2008 is considerable, including the expansion of the Baltic pipeline system, the de-bottlenecking of the Novorossiysk export facilities, expansion of rail-fed facilities at Vysotsk, Kaliningrad and Varandey, new capacity on the northern leg of the Druzhba pipeline system feeding Plock, and the potential reversal of the Adria to Druzhba pipeline. Although political, financial and fiscal uncertainties could undermine these, if all reached fruition export capacity could rise by 500kbpd between 2004 and 2008. Thus limits to export capacity growth may prove less of a check on Russian crude production from 2004-8 than had seemed likely, the report suggested, although it acknowledged that this might be more problematic in the longer-term, since it would depend on the speed with which new provinces were developed. Moreover, to ensure sustainable strong production growth through end-decade and the diversification of export markets would require decisions soon on key 1mbpd-plus export trunk-line projects, the report noted.[87]

Most experts and Russian officials argue that to increase production and enhance the oil reserve base and export capacity, major financial and expertise investment is necessary. One estimate given by the Russian Deputy Minister of Natural Resources Pyotr Sadovnik was of $65 billion to explore and put into operation gas and oil fields in northwest Russia alone through 2020, of which $5bn would be spent in exploration, approximately $50bn in operation and $10bn in pipelines.[88] The IEA estimates suggest that to maintain and develop Russia's energy infrastructure, investment of just under $1 trillion is necessary until 2030.[89] It is not simply cash that is necessary – Russia is considered to lack experience and means for the necessary exploration and operation in such harsh climes, for example deep water drilling and advanced offshore development, and to lack the latest equipment necessary for arctic exploration.[90]

As experts point out, though, forecasts of production depend as much on political as on technical considerations.[91] The political and business atmosphere in Russia has been ambiguous and dynamic since the collapse of the USSR – which has undermined the investment climate. If it is possible to argue that there has been greater political stability under President Putin, there have also been continuing political problems, including interference and uncertainty. Aside from the YUKOS case,[92] this has affected both investment and transport. Administrative questions remain about private property and huge capital outlays are unattractive in such an atmosphere – as one commentator has phrased it, investment requires a 'new appetite for risk'.[93] Russian experts note that due investment decisions are being held back. Although new tax decisions are positive, they have not clearly come into force.[94] Companies are also being threatened with the revocation of licences for exceeding maximum levels of production specified in the licence agreements, yet these maximum levels of oil production are based on the oil production technologies of the 1980s.[95]

There have also been clashes between private companies and state monopolies over the construction of pipelines. A consortium of Russian private companies sought to build a direct pipeline from Western Siberia to Murmansk to export oil to the US market. This however encountered serious opposition from Transneft, putting the pipeline in doubt.[96] One explanation for state authorities opposing private oil pipelines is that control over the pipelines is the only lever of influence over the oil firms.[97]

Finally, there is also an important inefficiency in the Russian oil sector. If experts consider that the oil industry is beginning to settle down in Russia and greater attention is now being given to exploitation of resources rather than industry structure and acquisition, questions remain about its structure. The two most prominent of these are whether the big companies are the most efficient vehicles for the exploitation of resources and maximisation of shareholder wealth and whether the industry's narrow and concentrated nature around a few giant companies obstructs long-term maximisation of supply. Big companies will not produce smaller fields and smaller reservoirs in larger fields and may leave them fallow. The second tier of smaller companies which would have exploited them is shrinking as it is being bought up by the big companies. According to one expert, this means that 'low-cost and more sustainable ... augmentation of supply is forsaken'.[98]

Thus, due to geology and geography on one hand and exploitation problems on the other, Russian oil production should not be expected necessarily to continue the strong growth shown since the late 1990s. There is a danger of either a lag time gap between the exhaustion of proved reserves (one expert notes that even if it were possible and attractive to invest such money, it is not likely that rewards would be reaped within five years)[99] and another strong growth period, or a more persistent decline over time. More probable, given the geography and costs, is decelerating growth, followed by a plateau which can be held for a number of years, followed by a slow decline in production levels.[100]

Simply, Russia holds a huge volume of physical oil, but much of it is uneconomic; and if Moscow promotes greater production and exports to feed its budget, 'technical, economic and political constraints bound this pursuit'.[101] It is also heavily dependent on world oil prices. There is little consensus about the size of Russian reserves and their economic viability. The size of reserves clearly varies with exploration and new technological development. Moreover, to reiterate, Russian oil reserves are a state secret. The reserves of private companies are also murky: when large companies re-valued and increased their stated reserves, this was more to do with acquisition of other smaller oil companies and stapling their reserves on to those of the bigger companies than finding new reserves to exploit. If production is unlikely to fall in the short-to-medium term, consumers cannot afford to be complacent about importing increasing amounts of Russian oil.

Third Party Competition for Russian Oil and Russian Pricing Behaviour

Given the finite nature of Russian oil production, one final point should be highlighted – competition for Russian oil. This of course is a vast issue, encompassing the Black Sea and Caspian and wider NIS regions, and can barely be broached here.[102] Nonetheless, the significant growth of demand for oil in China and India and their interest and investment in Russia has consequences for the EU. This growth in demand is already well documented, but for illustration, BP's Annual Statistical Review shows that Chinese growth alone was approximately 900,000 bpd in 2004. Other analyses suggest that China alone has accounted for approximately one third of the increase in consumption, making it the second largest oil consumer in the world and that China and India may both need to double their oil requirements by 2030.[103]

To meet their increased consumption, China, Japan and India have all been negotiating deals with Moscow to increase their access to Russian oil.[104] One analyst has noted that the Chinese were rumoured to have financed Rosneft's purchase of Yuganskneftgaz, and China reportedly paid a $6.6bn loan for the long-term pre-purchase of oil.[105] This has led to the drawing up of plans for pipeline construction to the Pacific.[106] LUKOIL began exporting oil to China in November-December 2004.[107] Thus, according to Khristenko, export of Russian fuels to Asia and Pacific countries may rise six-fold by 2015.[108]

It is worth highlighting, however, that the main competition for Russian oil may come from the USA. Some analyses have noted that growth in the Chinese and Indian economies is likely to fluctuate. China's share of world oil consumption, for example, remains below 8%, much smaller than that of the USA – even assuming continued robust growth, Goldman Sachs estimates that China will remain a smaller consumer than the USA for decades (Russian experts concur).[109] Moreover, some argue that China's growth of 16% in 2004 is unsustainable – much of the rise was due to its overheating economy and is unlikely to be repeated.[110] Finally, should China's overall economy take a knock, oil consumption is likely to fall.[111] The USA is the major consumer on the world market and has begun to look to Russia as part of its diversification of supply strategy. Russian and US firms are cooperating in Russia, and Russian companies have assets in the USA.[112] A Russia-US relationship has also developed at the state level, with meetings of special working groups.[113]

Such advances suit Moscow, as it seeks to maximise exports on the one hand and diversify its markets to enhance export security.[114] None of these relationships have yet developed fully, but when they do, it will mean increased competition for Europe to gain a share of Russian oil. Some Russian experts have already noted that such plans have given rise to EU jealousy, with senior EU officials voicing their displeasure with Russian intentions to export energy eastward and to the USA.[115] Competition for Russian oil will drive up prices and pose problems for slower growing economies, especially should western Siberian oil be tapped to feed the Eastern pipeline while eastern Siberian deposits are being explored and developed.[116] The point is clear: although western Siberian reservoirs are still producing, they are mature fields unlikely to revisit peaks – and there will be a lag time before new reservoirs begin production. Yet during this time (i.e. during the next 5-10 years), this supply will be sought by more consumers. As has already been noted in one newspaper, excessive growth in demand in the USA and China is effectively imposing a tax on others by pushing world prices higher – increased demand could drive these prices higher still. Moreover, with little spare capacity in the world oil sector, rapid growth leaves markets vulnerable to disruption.[117]

In this regard, one final point deserves mention. Russia in 2004 was again the leading contributor to the increase in non-OPEC oil production. This has meant that Russia is increasingly considered to be a strategic counterweight to the Middle East for reserves and counter to the decline of the USA and United Kingdom as consumers. Russia's rise as a producer therefore is, in the words of one expert, 'the most influential new force in the world oil market since the empowerment of OPEC in the 1970s' – Russia is a fulcrum for world prices. Being both an ally and opponent of OPEC, Russia's willingness to export and support OPEC pricing is crucial to the future of world prices.[118]

It may be that 'aggressive collusion' among oil producers to protect prices is unlikely, particularly during a period of high oil prices.[119] However, should prices fall, not only will the importance of Russian production capabilities come to the fore, but the significance of the Russia-OPEC relationship will increase. Russia will have to decide on a coherent output strategy and therefore a strategy both for its own production and in relation to OPEC. Russia has to date been more independent of OPEC strategy, but Russian foreign policy is evolving, as is its energy strategy. As noted above, there are already signs of debate about production levels. It may be, however, that in order to lengthen the plateau of oil production and slow decline, decisions are taken in Russia not to seek to maximise production. Officials have argued that a push to exceed 10mbpd may speed exhaustion of resources and lead to a steeper decline in production, perhaps to 5mbpd by 2020. Thus the CEO of Transneft has called for a more controlled development of energy resources.[120] The implications of such a decline would be widely felt internationally, and have important ramifications for an EU consumer competing in a global market with China, India, Japan and the USA. Equally, a growth in domestic consumption will add to this competition and impact on Russian export capacity.[121]

Conclusions

Concerns about Russia using its energy resources as a "weapon" against the EU fall at the nexus of two popular litanies – fears about energy security and fears about Russia. Each magnifies the other. Myth and perception have played an important role, as has political agenda, and rigorous examination of the problem has often been eschewed in favour of received knowledge. Such fears cannot be dismissed out of hand in the medium-to-long term, but two points emerge from this paper. First, the important question of energy supplies is already a priority element of the EU-Russia relationship. If it has often been sluggish, the successful prioritisation of the issue by the UK this year has served to reinvigorate the dialogue and broaden the range of those with a vested interest. A clearer framework has now been established, with a wider range of people having a direct vested interest.

Second, the paper has argued that there are a number of more important potential problems in the relationship. Oil at acceptable prices cannot be guaranteed, even through diversification – the only way to achieve oil security is by increasing domestic efficiency and decreasing demand. External problems lie on tactical and strategic levels. Tactically, questions about transit should be addressed. Predominant concerns are potential sabotage of the main transit pipelines from Russia to the EU, and the impact of poor weather on transit. Pipeline protection (primarily against terrorist attack) is a potential area for cooperation between Russia and the EU – to date, there has been little cooperation between Russia and the EU in the military security dimension. This might provide an opportunity.[122] Equally, there could be further cooperation in enhancing transit in harsh climate. Some recent cut-offs have occurred not due to terrorist or political action, but bad weather.[123]

Strategically, much more attention should be paid on one hand to the evolving Russia-OPEC relationship, a potentially very important one for the future of world prices. On the other, an eye will need to be kept on the actions of the transit states themselves, to clarify the extent of any malfeasance by Russia. In this regard, care will have to be taken to distinguish between stoppages due to technical problems, economic issues such as the non-payment of legitimate debt by the transit states themselves to Russia and political problems. Effort will have to be made to understand Russian energy security needs – including the legitimate desire to export directly from its own territory.

Russia would be the main loser in any political cut off of oil supplies to the EU. The Russian economy, although gaining a measure of independence, is still highly dependent on earnings from the export of energy to its primary market – western Europe. Moreover, Russia has few other serious market options. Even building a pipeline infrastructure to the east coast poses problems – Moscow also fears a Chinese monopoly on Asia/Pacific exports.

But there is little evidence to suggest that Russia would seek to do this – to the contrary. Russia has sought to be a reputable international supplier – and a reputation, particularly one as fragile as Russia's, is easily spoiled. The evidence "against" Russia, even in some of its dealings with the NIS, suggests on one hand a very thinly veiled Russo-phobia under which umbrella Russia can credibly be blamed for almost anything without close examination and on the other a more hard-nosed economic approach from Russia more than any particular political willingness to use energy as a weapon.

Certainly, circumstances may change, particularly after Russia's presidency of the G8 or after the presidential elections of 2008. However, this is more likely to reflect an emerging energy security dilemma rather than any deliberate policy to threaten the EU: Russian concern about the EU diversifying away from it is likely to lead to enhanced Russian efforts to develop other markets, resulting in both sides diversifying away from each other to "protect" their energy security. Moreover, it seems that despite the existence of this interdependence, the EU has still brought up difficult subjects such as Chechnya at the negotiation table. Indeed, *pace* Skinner's argument, it is worth considering that if the EU continues to dominate Russian oil export quotas – and even increases them – it will be in a stronger position to apply more effective sanctions or boycotts against Russia in any major disagreement with Russia.

There is currently too little knowledge of the Russian oil sector in the West – and too much received wisdom, particularly after the YUKOS affair. Experts in the EU need to ask some searching questions about the state of the Russian oil sector. What is the best structure for the Russian oil sector? Does state control, inefficient as it may be, necessarily inhibit long-term oil production and export? (Although the answer to this may still be "yes", a more detailed analysis of how and why is necessary.) Do Westerners blame the Russian state for too many of the ills?[124] What are the complexities of the state-private sector clashes? Does the Russian oil sector need western investment?[125] If so, for how long – and what are the alternatives? What are the ramifications for the West if and when Russian state or private companies do not need Western involvement? Experts should be ready for such questions to throw up some uncomfortable answers.

Most importantly, a change in focus is necessary in energy security discussion. An atmosphere of calm analysis should be established. Sweeping statements and problematic arguments are often offered on faith, with little or no supportive evidence. Frequently energy security seems to be charged with and driven by a more obscure agenda: "threats" such as Russia "turning the taps off" seem to act as a Trojan horse for other issues.[126] The question needs to be clarified – what is being sought here? What threat? In several instances the terminology needs to be changed – particularly in the consumer-producer debate: terms such as "dependence" play into the hands of easily communicated doomsday beliefs and the impending catastrophe. There also needs to be a change in approach from "us (consumers) vs. them (foreign producers)". The implication of such mistrust will generate more problems than seeking to build effective and fruitful relations. Interestingly, discussions with this author have shown that individual concerns about the Russia-EU oil (and broader energy) security relationship – weather-caused transit problems, political leverage, sabotage – are often considered not to pose significant risks in the foreseeable future. However, when "energy security" and "Russia" are put together more broadly, the risk is often considered to be high – the sum of fears is much greater than the individual parts. This needs much clearer assessment, with more developed argument.

The energy security relationship is a key area in the EU-Russia relationship, since it is a real area of mutual importance rather than concocted political desire. The relationship has not been "politically securitised" – and it should not be allowed to become a pawn in wider EU-Russia political-security problems or the agenda of specific players on either side. Continued effort will have to be focused on establishing and developing the economics and technicalities of the relationship, and broadening the range of those with a vested interest (both business and state) in the progress of the relationship.

Endnotes

[1] As the EU enlarges to incorporate states with relatively high economic growth rates, energy demand is predicted to grow by approximately 2% every year until 2020. *Energy: Let Us Overcome Our Dependence*, European Commission Green Paper, 2002. Luxembourg: Office for Official Publications of the European Communities, 2002. pp.2-3,9.

[2] *The Energy Dialogue Between the European Union and the Russian Federation between 2000 and 2004*, Communication From the Commission to the Council and the European Parliament. Brussels, COM (2004) 777 Final, 13/12/2004. p.2.

[3] Ibid, pp.2, 10.

[4] Green Paper. pp.4,13.

[5] *A Secure Europe in a Better World*. EU Security Strategy adopted by the European Council, December 2003. Paris: ISS, 2003.pp. 5-6.

[6] Prins, G. 'Lord Castlereagh's Return: the Significance of Kofi Annan's High Level Panel on Threats, Challenges & Change', *International Affairs*, Vol. 81, No.2, 2005. p.378.

[7] 'Taking on the Bear', *The Economist*, 7th May, 2005; Press Conference following EU-Russia summit, 4th October 2005; http://news.bbc.co.uk/1/hi/world/europe/4306770.stm. For an English language overview of some of the Russian press, see the BBC Monitoring Service translations at http://news.bbc.co.uk/1/hi/world/europe/4311340.stm. Interviews in London, Paris and Brussels, June, July & October 2005. It is worth noting that Chechnya was discussed at some length during the summit – for longer and more constructively than has usually been the case in the past.

[8] SVOP is a non-governmental forum for discussion among the Russian elite. See www.svop.ru for further details.

[9] Trety'akov, V. 'Pragmatizm vneshney politiki V. Putina', *Mezhdunarodnaya Zhizn'*, No.5, 2002. Nonetheless, he also stated that Russia seeks to be treated and regarded as an ally of the west in all spheres, including the export of energy fuels.

[10] Hill, F. *Beyond Co-dependency: European Reliance on Russian Energy*, US-Europe Analysis Series, The Brookings Institution, July 2005. www.brookings.edu

[11] Cited in 'Meet the Chief Executive of Kremlin Inc.', *The Guardian*, 06/07/05. It should be remembered that while Yavlinskiy is often cited as an important political figure by Western media because of his liberal programme, he is an opposition politician with an obvious political agenda.

16

[12] Fredholm, M. *The Russian Energy Strategy & Energy Policy: Pipeline Diplomacy or Mutual Dependence?* CSRC Paper 05/41, September 2005. p.3. www.da.mod.uk/csrc

[13] Rogozin cited in Hill, op. cit.; Official interviews with this author, June & July 2005.

[14] Interviews London, Paris, Brussels and Moscow, June & July 2005.

[15] For good background discussions, see Mitchell, J.V. *Renewing Energy Security*. London: RIIA, 2002 & Victor, D. G. & N. M. Victor, 'Axis of Oil?', *Foreign Affairs*, Vol.82. no.2, March/April 2003. The protection of the environment is an important element of energy security but one which falls outside the remit of this paper. For information on this subject with particular focus on Russia and Russia's ratification of the Kyoto Protocol, see Golub, A. & B. Muller, 'Kyoto's Future Lies in Putin's Hands', *Moscow Times*, 05/08/04 and Korppoo, A., Karas, J. & M. Grubb (eds.) *Russia and the Kyoto Protocol: Opportunities and Challenges*. London: RIIA/Chatham House, 2005 (forthcoming).

[16] This largely means protection of infrastructure, which is vulnerable to sabotage. An attack on just a few key terminals, shipping lanes (which are already congested), ports or pipelines could have devastating results for world oil supplies. Lovins, A.M. et al. *Winning the Oil Endgame: Innovations for Profits, Jobs & Security*. Snowmass: Rocky Mountain Institute, 2005. p.10. It is worth remarking that the pipeline system between Russia and Western Europe should in this respect be considered a potential terrorist target. Attempts to sabotage pipelines have already been made, for example at Manas in April 2004. Blandy, C.W. *Chechnya After Beslan*. CSRC Paper 04/27, September 2004. p.12. www.da.mod.uk/csrc

[17] Roberts, J. *Energy as a Security Challenge for the EU*, Paris: ISS, 2005. Forthcoming. p.4.

[18] For a good conspectus of the peak camp argument, see www.odac-info.org. The Oil Depletion Analysis Centre is a British think tank. Deffeyes, K. *Hubbert's Peak: The Impending World Oil Shortage*. Oxford: Princeton University Press, 2001.

[19] 'Oil in Troubled Waters – A Survey of Oil', *The Economist*, 30th April, 2005; Mitchell, p.10; Davies, P. & P. Weston, 'Oil Resources: A Balanced Assessment', *The CEPMLP Online Journal*, Vol.6, No.15. 2000.

[20] *UK International Priorities: The Energy Strategy*, London: FCO. p.13. http://www.fco.gov.uk/Files/kfile/Energy_Report_281004,0.pdf. It will be noted that officially the UK is closer to the "optimist" camp than the "peak" camp. Indeed, interviewees suggest that UK energy needs for the short to medium term are sustainable geologically and politically – the vast majority of UK gas and oil being imported from stable and friendly states. However, the term the 'next few decades' is remarkably vague.

[21] 'Oil in Troubled Waters'.

[22] Skinner, R & R. Arnott, 'The Oil Supply and Demand Context for Security of Oil Supply to the EU from the GCC Countries', Report, WPM 29. Oxford: Oxford Institute for Energy Studies, 2005. p.24. The authors draw on and refer to a number of sources to outline the various understandings of energy security. They also draw attention to environmental aspects of energy security.

[23] For fuller discussions of this, see Skinner, R. *Energy Security and Producer – Consumer Dialogue: Avoiding a Maginot Mentality*, Presentation to Government of Canada Energy Symposium, 28/10/05. www.oxfordenergy.org; Yeomans, M. *Oil*. London: New Press, 2004; Lovins et al., p.17; Victor & Victor, pp.51, 57; 'The Real Trouble with Oil', *The Economist*, 30/04/05.

[24] Rail exports travel via the Zabaykalsk (Russia-Chinese border) and Naushki (Russia-Mongolia border) railway stations, and are run by East Siberian Railway, a subsidiary of the state company Russian Railways. The construction of an eastbound oil pipeline is considered one of the most important tasks facing Russia's oil sector, according to Gennadi Shmal, the President of the Russian Union of Oil and Gas Producers. 'Union of Russia's Oil and Gas Producers Says Oil Exports in Danger', www.mosnews.com 16/03/05.

[25] Skinner & Arnott, p.25

[26] Grace, J. *Russian Oil Supplies: Performance and Prospects*. Oxford: OUP (for the Oxford Institute for Energy), 2005. p.178.

[27] See Ibid, appendix II.

[28] Arguments that Russia poses a threat often rely on such secrecy and obscurity, arguing that there is "little or no presentable evidence but it is happening".

[29] Skinner, 'Energy Security and Producer-Consumer Dialogue'. Skinner points out that most supply interruptions have been internal, caused by domestic political and technical problems – in the UK and France, it has usually been industrial action that has cut off

energy supplies through blockade, or technical problems reflecting lack of investment regulatory failure or cost cutting.

[30] Yeomans, p.143; Smith, K.C. *Russian Energy Politics in the Baltics, Poland and Ukraine*. Washington: CSIS, 2004. pp.ix, 5; Drezner, D. 'Allies, Adversaries, and Economic Coercion: Russian Foreign Economic Policy Since 1991' *Security Studies*, Vol.6, No.3, 1997; Abdelal, R. *Interpreting Interdependence: Energy and Security in Ukraine and Belarus*. CSIS Working Paper, July 2002; Oldberg, I. 'Foreign Policy Priorities Under Putin: A Tour d'Horizon', pp.38-9 & Hedenskog, J. 'Filling the Gap: Russian Security Policy Towards Belarus, Ukraine and Moldova Under Putin', p.147, both in Hedenskog, J. et al. (eds.) *Russia as a Great Power: Dimensions of Security Under Putin*. London: Routledge, 2005; Leijonhielm, J. & R. Larsson, *Russia's Strategic Commodities: Energy and Metals as Security Levers*. Oslo: Swedish Defence Research Agency, FOI, 2004. pp.129-30.

[31] See, for example, Smith, p.viii

[32] Abdelal.

[33] Ibid.

[34] Smith, p.5.

[35] Ibid, p.30.

[36] Myers Jaffe, A. & R.A. Manning, 'Russia, Energy and the West', *Survival*, Vol.43, No.2. Summer 2001. p.146.

[37] Fredholm, p.18; J. Robinson West, 'The Future of Russian Energy', *The National Interest*, Summer 2005. p.126.

[38] Rosneft and Transneft are the exception, since they are state monopolies. The complexities of Russian decision-making are manifest. For a good introduction, see Lo, B. & D. Trenin, *The Landscape of Russian Foreign Policy Decision Making*. Moscow: Carnegie Centre, 2005. One interviewee suggested that Russian decision-making processes were simply too disorganised for energy to be used effectively as a weapon by the state.

[39] This paper does not seek to address measures taken by the USSR to prevent secession/independence movements at the end of the 1980s/beginning of the 1990s.

[40] Fredholm, p.22; Interviews, London, Moscow, Brussels, June & July 2005.

[41] Victor Khristenko, Russia's Deputy Prime Minister (now Russian Minister for Energy and Industry) and Francois Lamoureux, the Commission's Director General for Energy and Transport.

[42] Working groups were to address energy strategies, technology transfers, investments and energy efficiency.

[43] Joint EU Presidency and European Commission Press release on the EU - Russia Permanent Partnership Council on Energy, 3rd October 2005, London. http://www.europa.eu.int/comm/external_relations/russia/summit_10_05/ip05_1218.htm , interviews, Moscow, Brussels, London, June, July, October 2005.

[44] www.europa.eu.int; www.technologycentre.org; Communication from the Commission to the Council, 13/12/04 on Energy Dialogue; EU-Russia Energy Dialogue, 5th Progress Report, November 2004, 'Putin, Blair Positive on Russia-EU Ties' www.mosnews.com 04/10/05.

[45] www.europa.eu.int; Russia-EU Energy Dialogue Synthesis Report No.1, September 2001, Summit Press Release, 04/10/05.

[46] Interviews with EU officials, June & July 2005.

[47] Lynch, D. *Russia Faces Europe*, Chaillot Paper No.60. Paris: ISS, 2003, p.65. In fact, as Lynch points out, both sides are *demandeurs* in the negotiations.

[48] Grigoriev, L. & A Chaplygina, 'Looking into the Future: The Energy Dialogue Between Russia and the European Union', *Russia in Global Affairs*, May 2003. http://eng.globalaffairs.ru/numbers/3/476.html

[49] Interview with Julian Lee, Senior Energy Analyst, Centre for Global Energy Studies, August 2005. Here it is worth noting internal disagreement and between producers and transporters. Producers are seeking to boost export, and have criticised Transneft for the inadequate infrastructure. To deflect such criticism, Transneft the pipeline monopoly, has argued for a proposal to restrict oil production and follow the example of OPEC by establishing state control over oil output. 'Pipeline Monopoly Suggests Russian OPEC', www.mosnews.com 23/03/04. It is also worth noting the differences in expectation of oil production capabilities, for example, 'Russia won't be able to increase oil production – Economic Minister', www.mosnews.com , 17/06/04 and 'Russia to increase oil production –

Russian Finance Minister', www.mosnews.com 24/05/04. There seem to be ongoing differences between the Ministries for Natural Resources, Finance and Economics about legislation and planning.

[50] Leijonhielm, & Larsson, p.57; Smith, p.13; Putin cited in Paramonov & Strokov, p.7; J. Robinson West has noted that many Russian industries remain highly inefficient and rely on cheap energy to subsidise their operations. p.125.

[51] See, for instance, the Energy Dialogue's 3rd Progress Report, November 2002; Communication from the Commission to the Council, 13/12/04; www.delrus.cec.eu.int.

[52] Grigoriev & Chaplygina; Milov, V. *Russian Energy Policy Challenges*. Presentation, Moscow, February 2005; Baev, P. *Putin's European Project: Derailed or Set Back in Reformatting?*, PONARS Policy Memo, No. 331. November 2004. p.2.

[53] Leonard, M. *Why Europe Will Run the 21st Century*. London: The Fourth Estate, 2005. pp.79-80.

[54] BP Annual Statistical Review, 2005. p.12. www.bp.com/statisticalreview

[55] Skinner, 'Energy Security and Producer-Consumer Dialogue'; interviews in London, Paris and Moscow, June, July & October, 2005.

[56] Gorst, I. 'Russian Pipeline Strategies: Business vs. Politics', *The Energy Dimension in Russian Global Strategy*, J.A. Baker III Institute for Public Policy of Rice University, October 2004. p.3.

[57] Leijonhielm, & Larsson, pp.47, 50-1.

[58] Hill; Fredholm, p.13.

[59] Hill, op. cit.

[60] Ibid.

[61] Lynch, D. (ed.) *What Russia Sees*. Chaillot Paper No.74, Paris: ISS, p.119.

[62] A security dilemma emerges when one state, suspicious of military preparations by another, begins to make its own preparations in case the other intends to threaten it. In response, the former itself becomes increasingly suspicious, and prepares in turn for the inverse eventuality, beginning an arms race and an unstable relationship.

[63] Yeomans, p.115.

[64] Grace, p.213.

[65] Brunstad, B. et al. *Big Oil Playground, Russian Bear Preserve or European Periphery? The Russian Barents Sea Region Towards 2015*. Delft: Eburon Publishers, 2004. pp. 21-49.

[66] Grace, p.215.

[67] Production in 1994 was 6,419 thousand barrels per day, but then dropped to 6,288 in 1995, and again to 6,114 in 1996. An increase to 6,227 in 1997 was again followed by a decrease in 1998. *BP Annual Statistical Review*, 2004. This fall was due to a number of reasons, according to Russian experts, including the deterioration of explored reserves, the slow introduction of new development technologies, and a great number of wells standing idle. Gritsenko, A. et al. 'Oil and Gas of Russia in the XXI Century: Forecast of Production and Development of the Resource Base', *Journal of Mineral Resources of Russia*, No. 3, 2001. www.geoinform.ru/

[68] *BP Annual Statistical Review*, 2005. p.6.

[69] Lee, J. *Future Russian Oil Production: the CGES View*, presented at CERI Oil Conference March 2004. www.cges.co.uk

[70] 'Russia's Oil Output Hits Post-Soviet High', www.mosnews.com, 03/10/05.

[71] Gaddy, C. 'Americanski vzglyad na russkuyu neft'', *Mezhdunarodnaya Zhizn'*, No.11, 2004; Grace, p.215.

[72] Lee, *Future Russian Oil Production*; Grace, p.4.

[73] Grace, p.219.

[74] See, for example, Konoplyanik, A.A. 'Is Oil Production Crisis Imminent in Russia?', *Journal of Mineral Resources of Russia*, 1/01. www.geoinform.ru

[75] Trutnev cited in Gorst, p.9.

[76] Cited in 'Union of Russia's Oil & Gas Producers Says Oil Exports in Danger', www.Mosnews.com 16/03/05.

[77] Interview with Lee; Grace, p.183.

[78] Ibid, p.183.

[79] Paramonov & Strokov, pp.3-4; Gaddy, 'The End of Russia's Oil Boom' Grace, p.215. Grace also points out that developing these fields entails addressing environmental protection concerns.

[80] Grace, pp.190, 205.

[81] Lee, *Future Russian Oil Production.*

[82] Grace, p.190.

[83] Victor & Victor, p.53. This is partly due to domestic causes, but also due to external geographical factors, such as congestion in the Bosphorous which limits marine traffic, and environmental considerations which have slowed infrastructure development in the Danish Straits. Milov.

[84] Gorst, p.5.

[85] US DOE Russia Country Paper.

[86] The IEA is an intergovernmental body committed to advancing security of energy supply, economic growth and environmental sustainability through energy policy co-operation.

[87] *IEA Oil Market Report: A Monthly Oil Market and Stocks Report*, 12/05/04. p.21. www.oilmarketreport.org

[88] 'Russia needs $65bn to explore its North-western oil and gas fields', RosBusiness Consulting, newsonline, 11/02/04, www.rbcnews.com

[89] Cited in Mandil, C. *Securing the Russia-European Energy Partnership.* www.iea.org/textbase/papers/2005/russia.pdf

[90] Leijonhielm & Larsson p.39. Many commentators note that this experience and technology can only come from the west. Although China and India are investing in Russia, they too lack such experience, skills and technology.

[91] Skinner; Lee, *Future Russian Oil Production*

[92] An early examination of the YUKOS case can be found in Volkov, V. *The YUKOS Affair: Terminating the Implicit Contract.* PONARS Policy Memo No.307. November 2003. If other Russian oil companies have professed greater loyalty to the regime since the YUKOS affair, it is still too early to view many of the ramifications of the proceedings.

[93] J. Robinson West, p.126.

[94] Interviews, October-November 2005. Since 2005, the state skims nearly 100% of the revenues over $25/barrel. This, in combination with other administrative questions means that the exploration and development of expensive oilfields and maintaining high production rates is not attractive – as one Russian expert put it 'progressive taxation + expensive alternative transport = profitless development of expensive oilfields'.

[95] Interview with Lee.

[96] Brunstad et al, pp.49-50. It is now considered by some Russian experts to be only a regional project for the export of Timan-Pechora oil rather than a new large-scale project for the export of oil from West Siberia. Indeed, the main initiators of the Murmansk pipeline have abandoned it.

[97] 'Pipeline Monopoly Suggests Russian OPEC'. Although this is clearly an important lever, the point lends colour to those who argue that private oil firms are independent of the state and not tools for directly exerting foreign influence. In contrast, Milov has argued that some businesses have been forced to make politically motivated, non-economic energy asset acquisitions on the territory of the FSU.

[98] Grace, p.222. A Russian expert has also noted that vertical integration has caused a stagnation in the Russian refining industry, which has become secondary business and uncompetitive.

[99] Skinner.

[100] Grace, p.216; Gritsenko, A.I., Krylov, N.A., Alenin, V.V. & V.P. Stupakov, 'Oil & Gas Of Russia in the XXI Century: Forecast of Production and Development of the Resource Base', *Journal of Mineral Resources of Russia*, www.geoinform.ru

[101] Grace, p.212.

[102] For good introductions to these issues, see Roberts, J. The Black Sea and European Energy Security' Presentation at 3rd Black Sea Energy Summit, October 2004; Guseinov, V. *Caspiiskaya neft: Ekonomika i geopolitika.* Moscow: Olma-Press, 2002.

[103] *BP Annual Statistical Review*; Lovins et al., p.2; Fredholm, p.1. Nandakumar, J. 'China's Energy Security and the Taiwan Factor', *CEPMLP online Journal*, Vol.15; Yeomans, p.108.

[104] Pilling, D. & I Gorst, 'Tokyo in threat to withdraw from $11bn oil pipeline', *Financial Times*, 30/04/05.

[105] J. Robinson West, p.127.

[106] Smith, p.15; Myers Jaffe & Manning, p.144.

[107] 'Russia's LUKOIL starts exports to China', www.mosnews.com 18/11/04.

[108] 'Russia to Boost Oil and Gas Production By 2015 – Minister', www.mosnews.com 31/10/05; see also 'Export of Russian oil to China to rise 1.5 times – Chinese Oil Chief', www.mosnews.com 09/06/05.

[109] Milov.

[110] One senior businessman remarked in interview that at such a rate the Chinese economy would double every four years.

[111] 'Oil in Troubled Waters', p.6.

[112] 'Russia's LUKOIL to increase its presence in US', www.mosnews.com 25/05/05.

[113] Victor & Victor, p.48.

[114] Myers Jaffe & Manning, p.144. In this regard, it should be noted that Moscow is not just concerned about dependence on the European market. Moscow is also concerned about China developing a monopoly in the East – Moscow hopes to decrease dependence on Beijing by diversifying exports to the wider Asia Pacific market. Lo, B. 'A Fine Balance - The Strange Case of Sino-Russian Relations', *Russie.CEI.Visions*, No.1, April 2005. p.5. www.ifri.org

[115] Arbatov, A., Feygin, V. & V. Smirnov, 'Unrelenting Oil Addiction', *Russia in Global Affairs*, April – June 2005. http://eng/globalaffairs.ru/numbers/11/914.html

[116] Gorst, p.15; Smith, p.15; Yeomans, p.118; Lovins et al., p.22.

[117] 'The Oiloholics', *The Economist*, 27/08/05.

[118] Grace, pp.1, 223.

[119] Mitchell, p.18. This is for a number of reasons, including very unevenly resource distribution, different capabilities for and interests in expanding supply. Mitchell points out that countries with less potential volume are more interested in slower demand growth and higher prices that those that can increase revenues more by expanding volumes at current prices than by restraint.

[120] 'Russian Oil Companies Makes the Most of High Oil Prices', www.mosnews.com 21/05/04.

[121] 'Russia to Play a Key Role in International Energy Security', www.mosnews.com 23/11/04.

[122] Although this has been mentioned by Russia, two points are likely to undermine this: pipeline can be quickly and easily replaced. Colombia provides a good illustration of quick pipeline repair – there have been frequent efforts to sabotage pipelines but with little lasting success. Interview with Lee. Second, militaries are shy of trying to protect hundreds of miles of infrastructure.

[123] Shipments from the Black Sea port of Novorosiysk were reduced due to stormy weather. 'Russia's Output Hits Post-Soviet High', www.mosnews.com 03/10/05. This is also feasible in the Baltic Sea.

[124] If the state is not keen on foreign companies becoming widely involved, it may also be argued that private Russian companies do not want the competition.

[125] Some experts in the west argue that the Russians have already profited handsomely from Western investment and by hiring western experts and need less and less involvement

[126] This point arose in discussion with Robert Skinner.

Dr. Andrew Monaghan is a Visiting Lecturer in the Defence Studies Department, the academic branch of the Defence Academy of Great Britain. He is also a Research Associate at the Conflict Studies Research Centre, part of the Defence Academy, and a Global Fellow at the Foreign Policy Centre, a think tank in London. He completed his doctorate in the Department of War Studies, King's College, London, from where he also holds an MA in War Studies. He can be contacted at andrewcm@hotmail.com

The author would like to thank the many experts and officials in London, Paris, Brussels and Moscow who agreed to be interviewed in preparation for this paper in the summer and autumn of 2005.

Want to Know More ...?

See:Grace, J. *Russian Oil Supply: Performance and Prospects.* Oxford: OUP, 2005.

Lynch, D. (ed.) *What Russia Sees.* Chaillot Paper No. 74. Paris: ISS, 2005.

Monaghan, A. 'From Plans to Substance: EU-Russia Relations During the British Presidency', *Russia.CEI.Visions*, August 2005. http://www.ifri.org/files/Russie/monaghan_english.pdf

For a map of existing and planned pipelines see http://www.transneft.ru/Shema/Shema.asp?LANG=EN

Disclaimer

ISBN 1-905058-48-9